Dressing the His Teddy Bea...

by Sheila Lile
photography by Sheila Lile

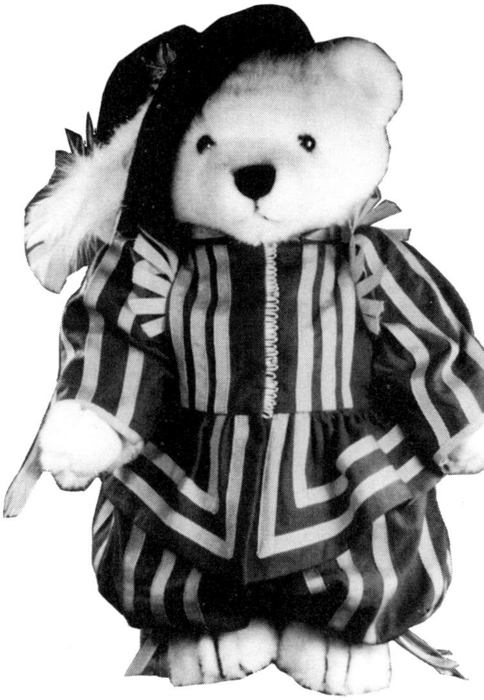

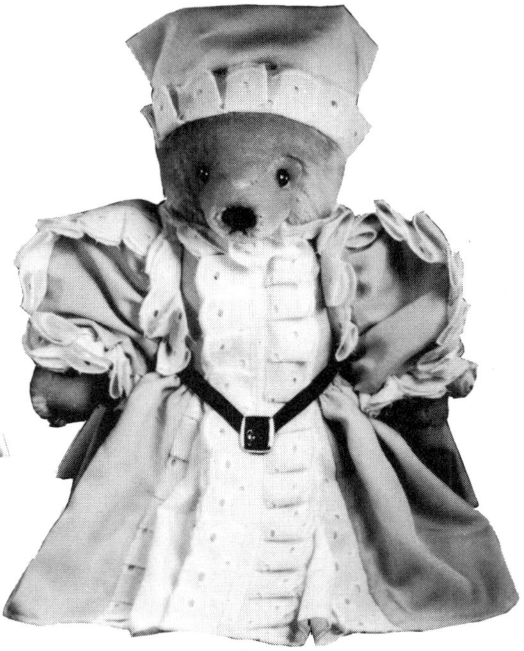

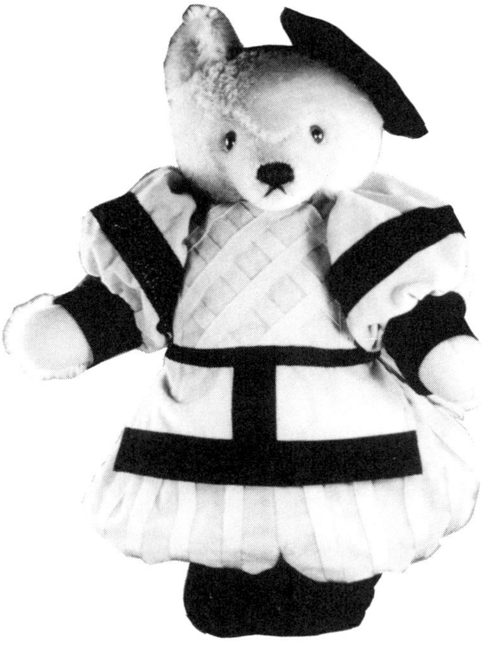

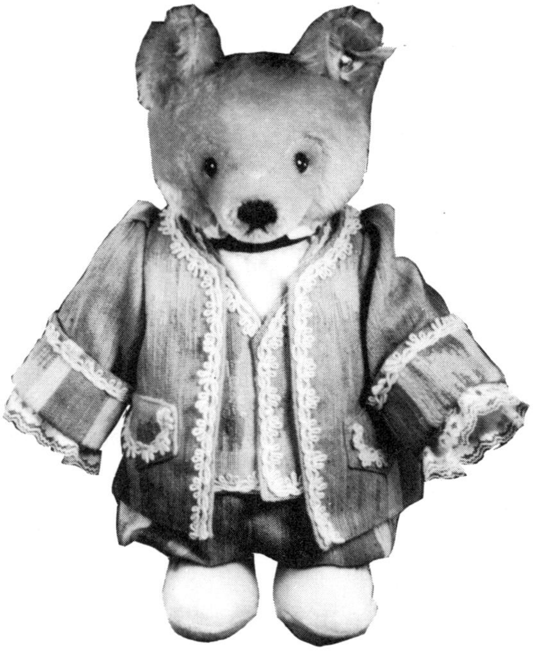

Published by Hobby House Press, Inc.
Cumberland, Maryland 21502

Additional copies of this book may be purchased at $5.95
from
HOBBY HOUSE PRESS, INC.
900 Frederick Street
Cumberland, Maryland 21502
or from your favorite bookstore or dealer.
Please add $1.25 per copy postage

© 1988 Sheila Lile

All rights reserved. No part of this book may be reproduced or utilized in any form or by any means, electronic or mechanical, including photocopying, recording, or by any information storage and retrieval system, without permission in writing from the publisher. Inquiries should be addressed to Hobby House Press, Inc., 900 Frederick Street, Cumberland, Maryland 21502.
Printed in the United States of America

ISBN:0-87588-332-X

TABLE OF CONTENTS

1620s King Charles 4
Tudor 12
Elizabethan Man 22
French 18th Century 30

General Sewing Instructions

1. First of all, read the instructions before sewing. This is very important. I write the instructions as I sew the garment so it makes the sewing easier for you if you follow step by step.
2. The seam allowance is marked on each pattern piece. Usually it is 1/4in (0.65cm). It is very important when you are sewing to use the correct seam allowance, especially when sewing small garments.
3. I use the term baby hem in my instructions. This means to turn up the fabric once and turn up again and stitch in place. It may be 1/8in (0.31cm) or 1/4in (0.65cm), usually the first.
4. When I refer to the self fabric, this always means the outer fabric or the fabric you cut the outfit out in to be seen on the outside. The linings will most often be the same fabric as the self unless, of course, you are working in a heavy fabric. In this book I do have some specific instructions for satin or slick linings. They tend to fit the bears better.
5. When you buy elastic, always look for a good tight elastic.
6. I use the term notches in my instructions. This is a garment industry term and they will be seen on my patterns as the little short lines on the pattern used to match up two pattern pieces. I put a little top on the line so they look like "T's."
7. Try to notch no further than 1/8in (0.31cm) in when cutting your fabric. You have only 1/4in (0.65) seam allowance so any more than this could ruin your garment.
8. You may have an overlock machine and will want to overlock the garments to make them clean. You can zigzag also. I have a few patterns that have to be zigzagged so be careful when you sew and read the instructions.
9. Not all pattern pieces fit on one page in a book of this style so just connect the letters to make the complete piece.
10. Always take your time when you sew and you will have a nice garment.
11. Please check your bear for variance in measurements.
12. Happy sewing and enjoy the book and please be creative.

1620s KING CHARLES OUTFIT

This 16in (41cm) Dakin Anniversary Teddy Bear is dressed in a shirt and pants with ribbon trim. A hat with feathers top it off.

FABRIC AND NOTIONS:

45in (114cm) fabric (jacket and pants)	1yd (91cm)
Felt (hat)	¼yd (23 cm)
Buttons (amount will depend on the number of loops you put on the front jacket)	
Feathers (hat)	3
1/4in (.65cm) ribbon	9yd (823 cm)
1/16in (.15cm) ribbon (loops on front jacket)	1yd (91cm)
1/4in (.65cm) elastic	3/4yd (69cm)
Thread to match	
1/4in (.65cm) foldover bias	1/2yd (46cm)

PANTS:
1. Sew the grosgrain ribbon onto the pants at the markings. (See pattern.)
2. Sew the front and back seams. Press.
3. Sew the crotch seam. Clip curves at the crotch. Press.
4. Press waist and pant leg hems under 1/8in (.31cm). Turn under again 1/2in (1cm) and stitch leaving an opening to insert elastic. Insert 12in (31cm) of elastic into the waist and 6in (15cm) into each pant leg. Stitch ends of elastic closed and close the opening.
5. Cut 10, 3in (8cm) strips of ribbon. Sew five on each side of the pants at the hem on the inside and let the ends hang out.

JACKET:
1. Sew loops onto the center front jacket using the 1/16in (.15cm) ribbon. You may also find some trim you like better than ribbon for the loops.
2. With right sides facing, sew the shoulder seams together. Press seams open. Repeat on lining.
3. Sew the ribbon onto the front bodice.
4. Cut ribbon into 34, 2in (5cm) strips. Sew the strips of ribbon to the armhole between the notches. Lay them edges touching and work your way around the armhole of the bodice. After the sleeve is sewn, you can trim the ribbon so that it graduates from bottom to top at the shoulder seam.
5. Sew foldover bias to the sleeve hem. Sew the ribbon onto the length of the sleeve. (See pattern for markings.)
6. Shirr the sleeve to fit the armhole. Sew the sleeve into the armhole. Sew up the side seam.
7. With right sides facing, sew ends of the collar. Turn and press. Sew ribbon to the collar, cleaning the ends.
8. Sew collar to the neckline.
9. Sew side seams together on the peplum on the self and the lining. Press.
10. With right sides facing, sew around the peplum leaving the waist free. Turn and press.
11. Sew ribbon to the peplum.
12. Shirr the peplum waist to fit the bodice waist. Sew the peplum to the self bodice.
13. With right sides facing, sew lining bodice to self. Sew up the center back, around the neck and back down center back on the other side. Clip, turn and press.
14. Sew lining side seams and press. Fold lining hem under 1/4in (.65cm) and press. Hand-stitch to the waist to clean. Stitch lining armhole to the self armhole.
15. Sew on the buttons.
16. Cut the strips of ribbon just like for the sides of the pants and sew to the center of the sleeve hem.

HAT:
1. Lay hat band together at the ends (just touching) and zigzag together.
2. Sew band to the crown by laying the edges together and zigzagging.
3. Sew the brim to the band in the same fashion.
4. Add the feathers.

Dress your bear up and he is ready for a walk into the past.

1620s KING CHARLES OUTFIT
for 16in (41cm) Teddy Bear
HAT CROWN
Cut 1 felt

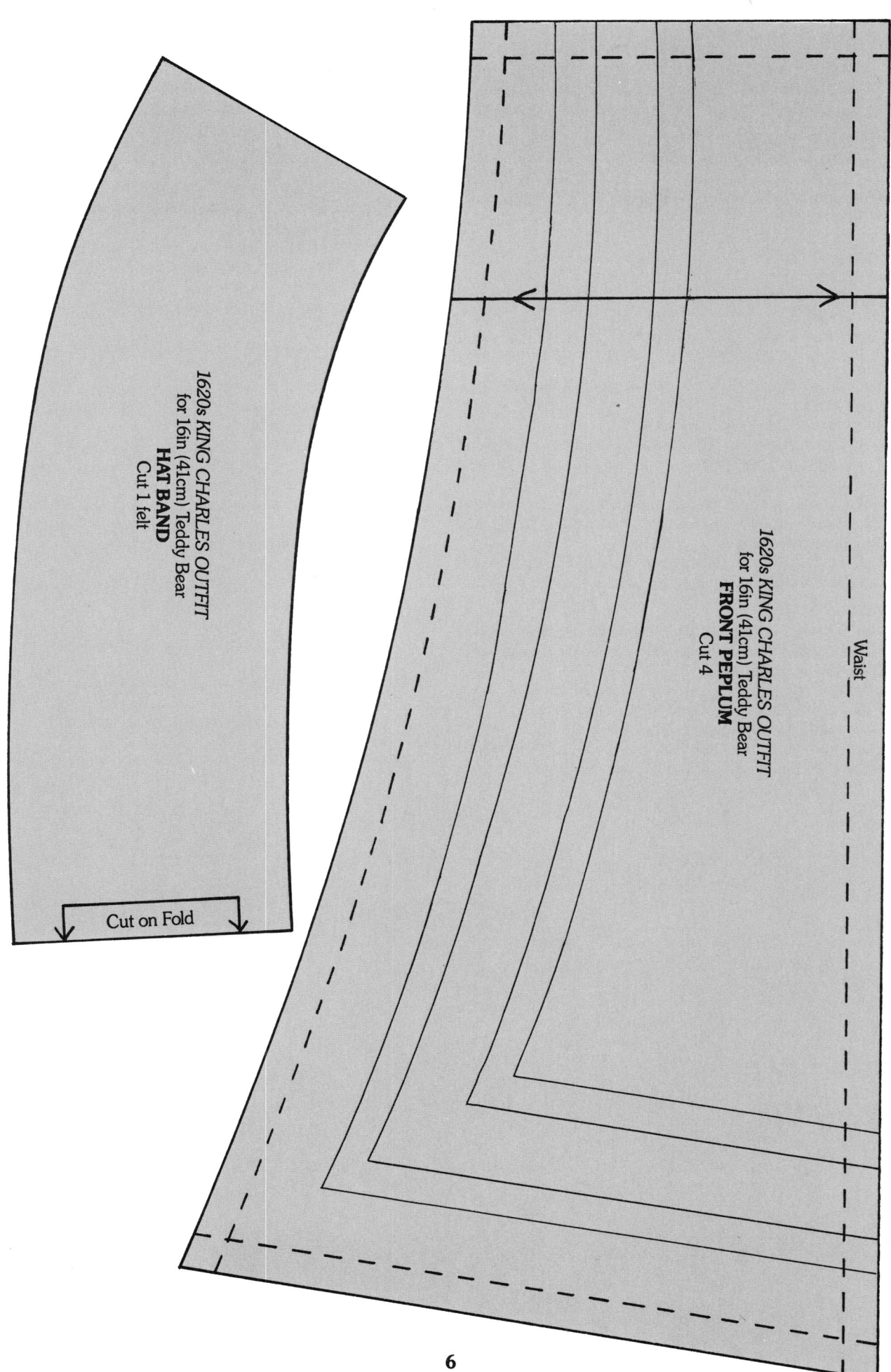

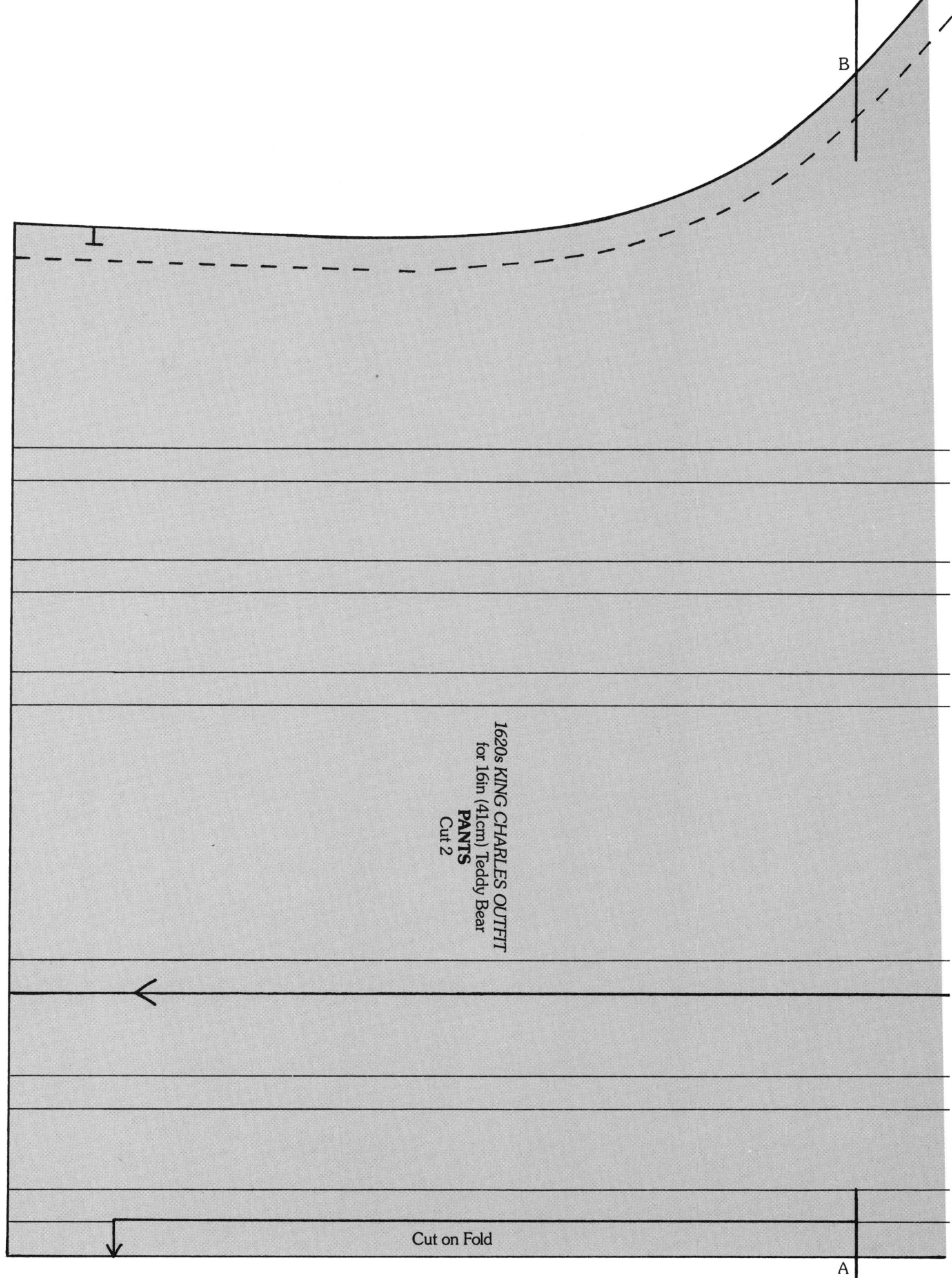

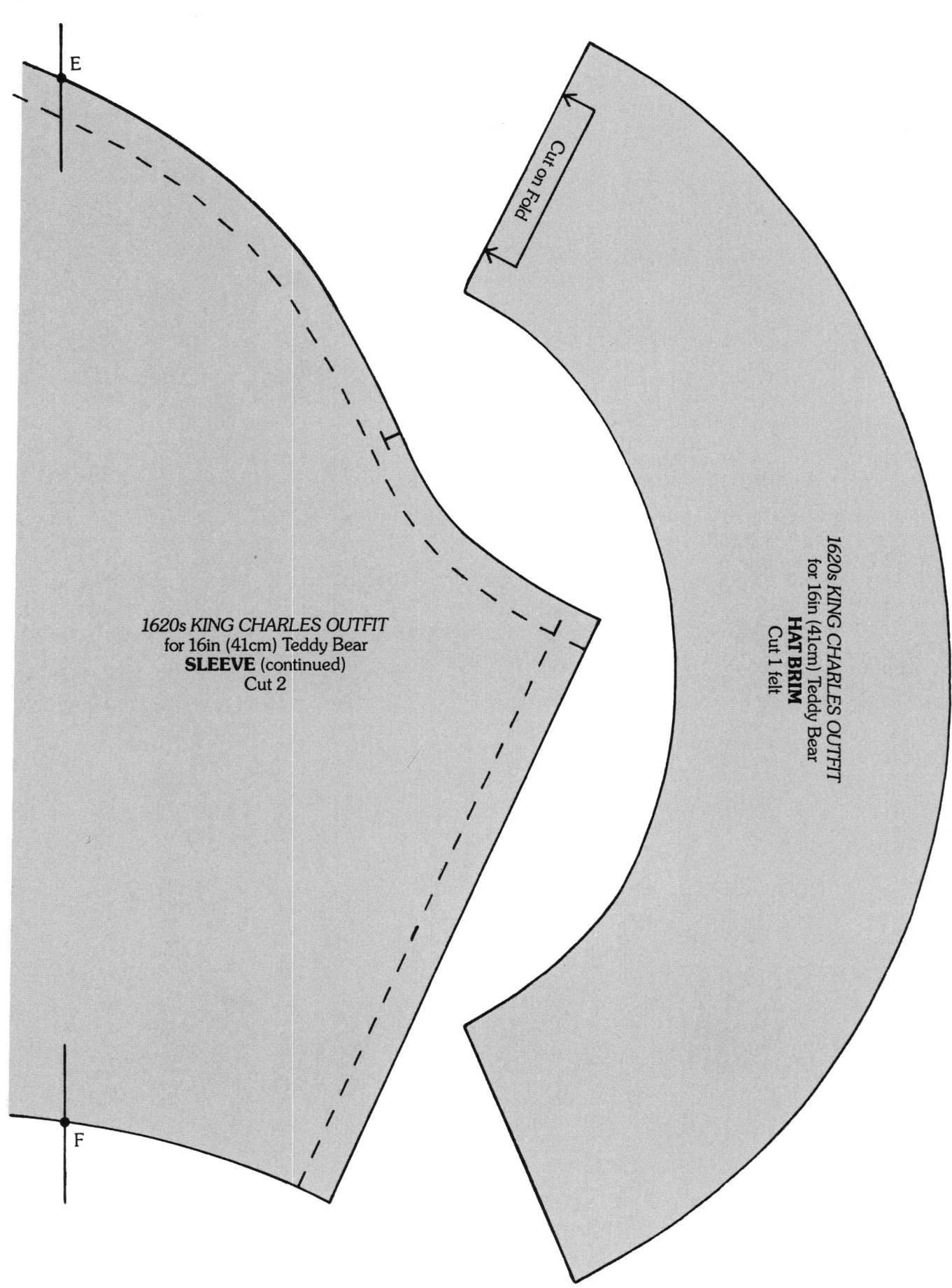

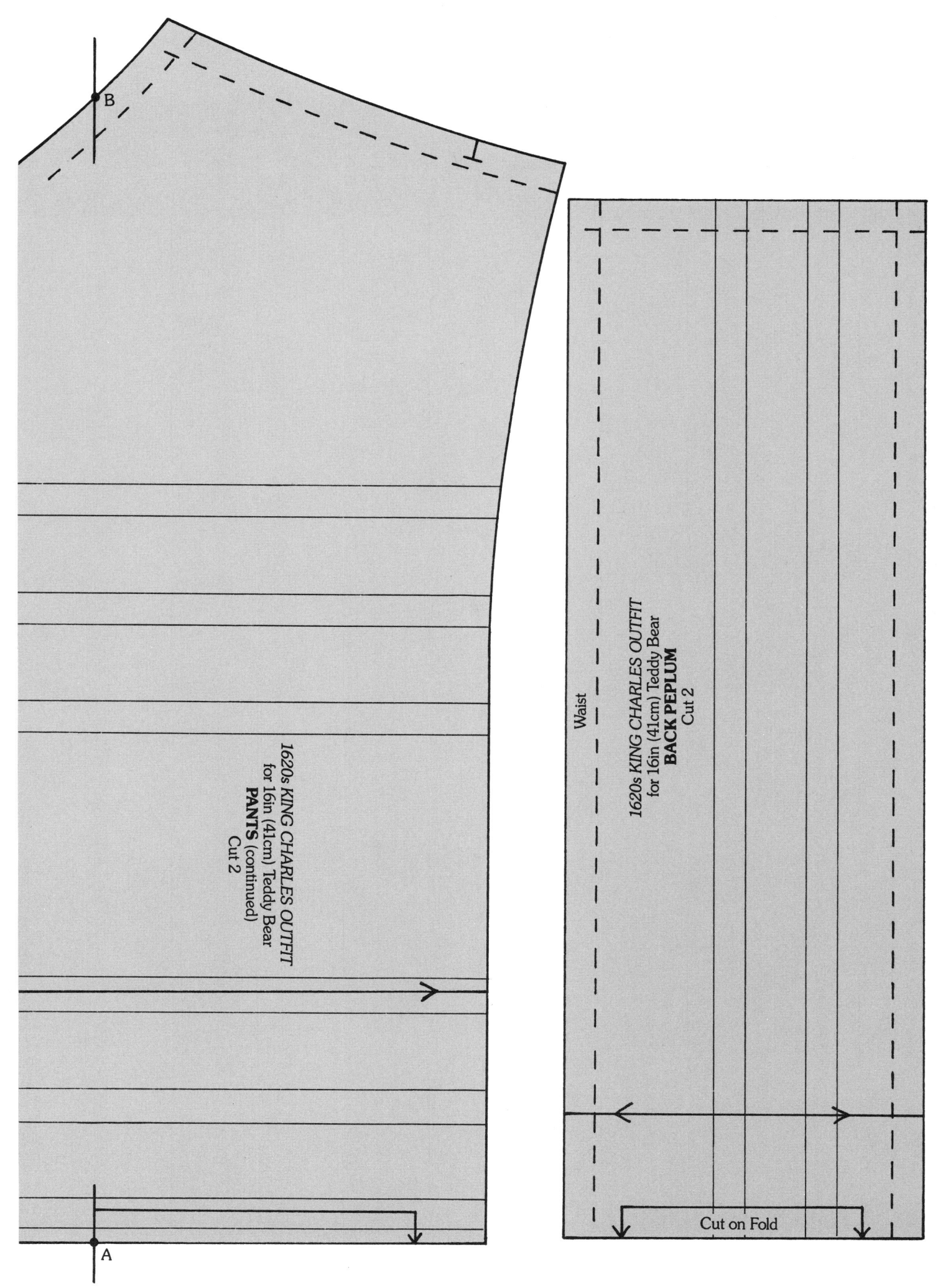

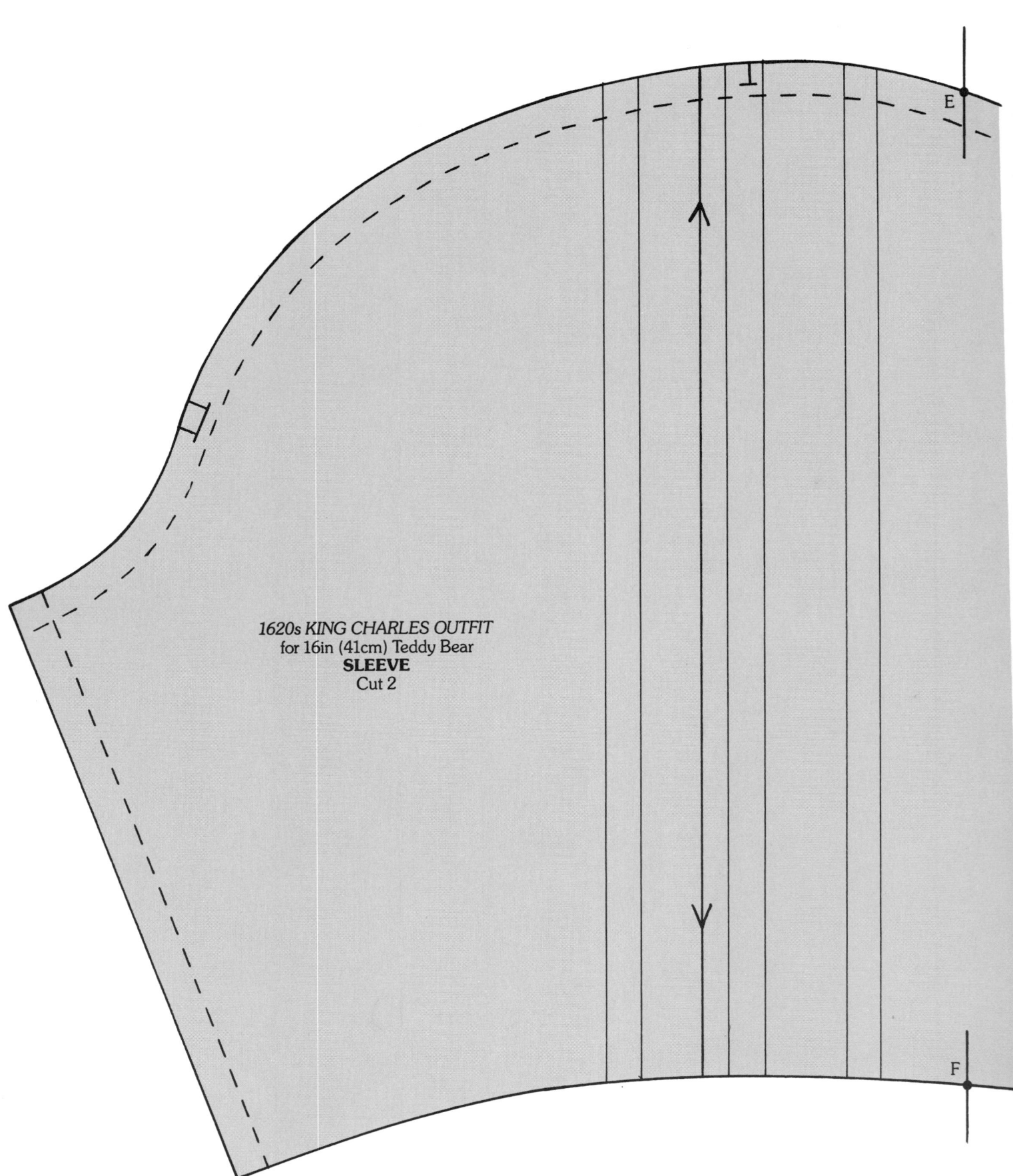

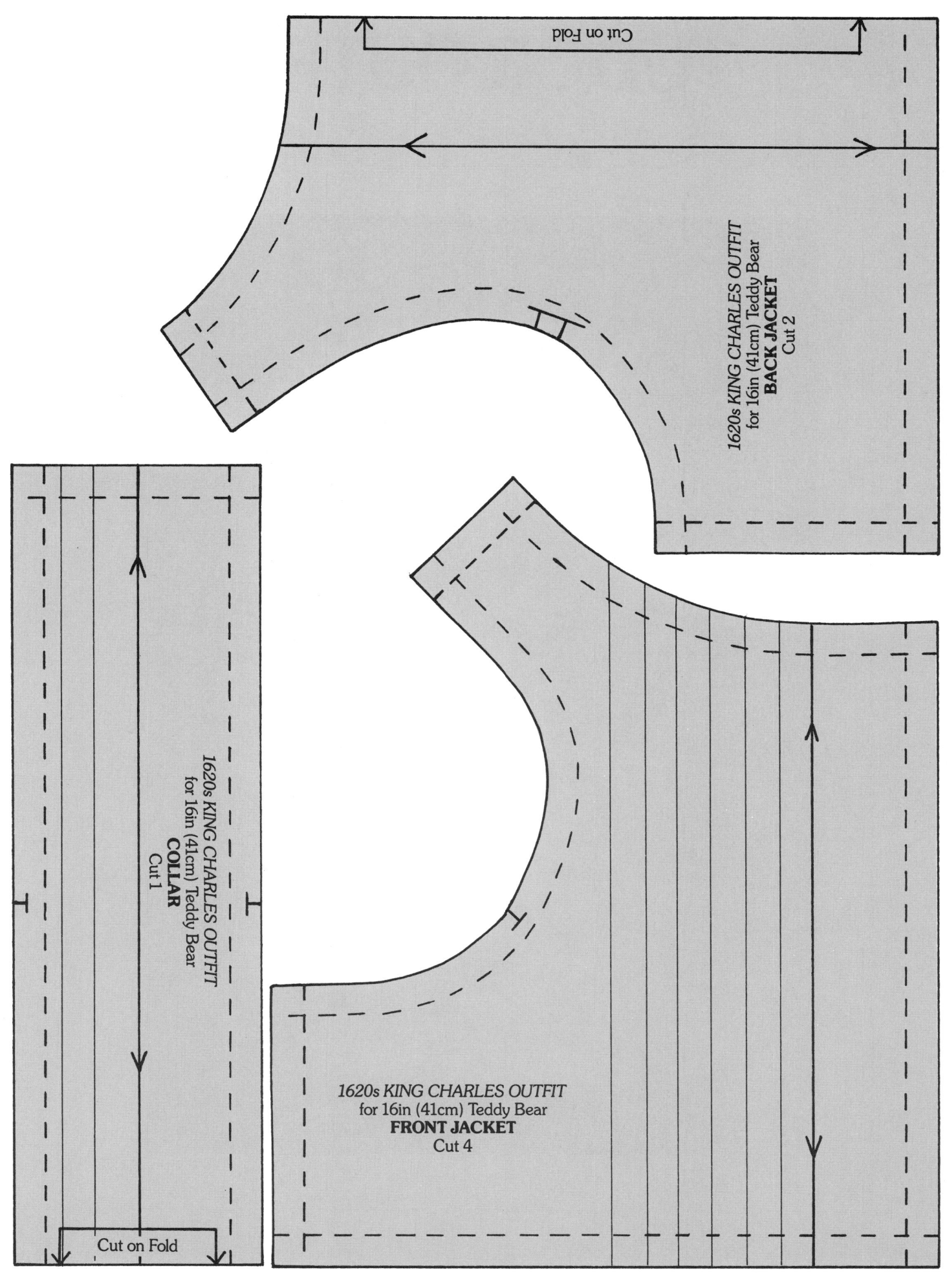

TUDOR OUTFIT

This 12in (31cm) Steiff Teddy Bear is dressed in a dress with pleated lace trim.

FABRIC AND NOTIONS:

45in (114cm) fabric (dress, lining)	1/2yd (46cm)
45in (114cm) contrasting fabric (hat, under skirt)	1/2yd (46cm)
1/4in (.65cm) ribbon (dress front)	1/3yd (31cm)
1/4in (.65cm) ribbon (waist tie)	1/2yd (46cm)
Pin or brooch	1
Thread to match	
Buttons/snaps	3
1¼in (3cm) wide flat lace (dress, hat)	8yd (732cm)
1/4in (.65cm) elastic	1/2yd (46cm)

DRESS:
1. Pleat all the lace with a 3-1 ratio. Do not press the lace.
2. Make pleats about 1in (2cm). I will refer to the pleated lace as the ruffle in these instructions.
3. Sew the ruffle to the center of each sleeve on the front sleeve. Press the seam only.
4. Sew the shoulder seams together on the self and lining. Press the seams open.
5. Sew the ruffle to the sleeve cap on the bodice between the notches. Turn the ends so that no raw edges show.
6. Shirr the sleeve to fit the armhole. Sew the sleeve into the armhole.
7. With right sides facing, sew the ruffle onto the edge of the sleeve with raw edges together. Stretch and sew elastic to the edge. Turn the ruffle down.
8. Sew the side seams and press. Sew ruffle to neck.
9. With right sides facing, sew lining to self. Sew up center back, around neck and back down center back on the other side. Turn and press.
10. Sew the side seams on the lining. Connect the armhole lining to the self. Stitch the waists together to hold in place on the bodice.
11. Baby hem the center back skirts separately.
12. Baby hem the skirt hems separately.
13. See the pattern and cut off the top skirt at the markings. This is a portion of the front.
14. On the front edge of top skirt sew the ruffle. Zigzag the seam and press.
15. Lay the two skirts together and shirr the waists to fit the bodice waist. Sew the skirt to the bodice.
16. Sew two ruffles together down the center front with raw edges together. Be sure to turn ends of lace so no raw edges show. Cover the raw edges at the center front with ribbon.
17. Sew on the snaps at the center back.

HAT:
1. Sew ruffle to one edge of hat.
2. Fold hat back with right sides facing and stitch ends, leaving a small opening to turn.
3. Turn and press.
4. Pin the hat to the bear's head when she wears it.

For the waist detail tack the ribbon at the "V" point on the front dress. Tie the ribbon at the back dress. Attach the pin or brooch to the front on top of the ribbon.

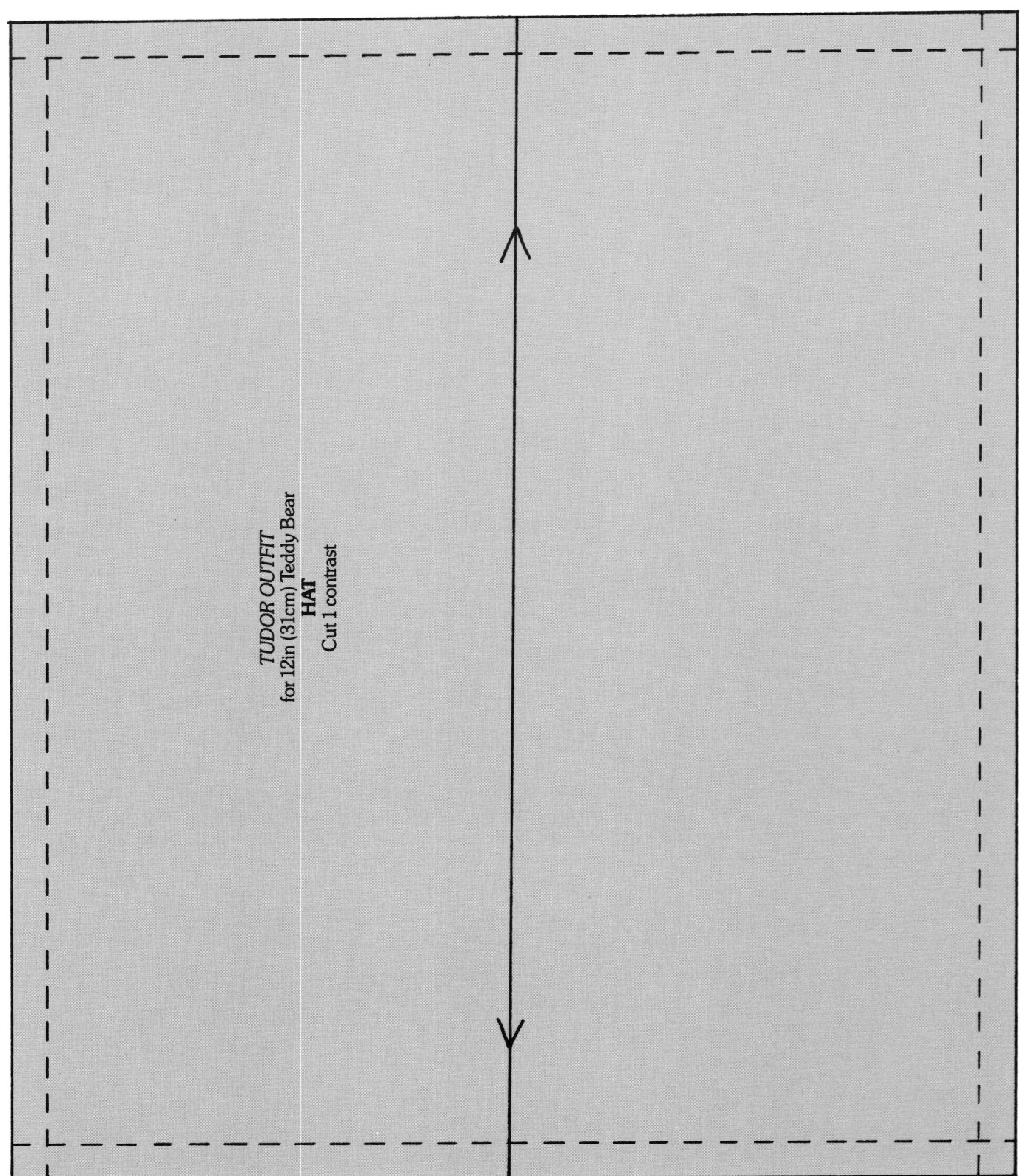

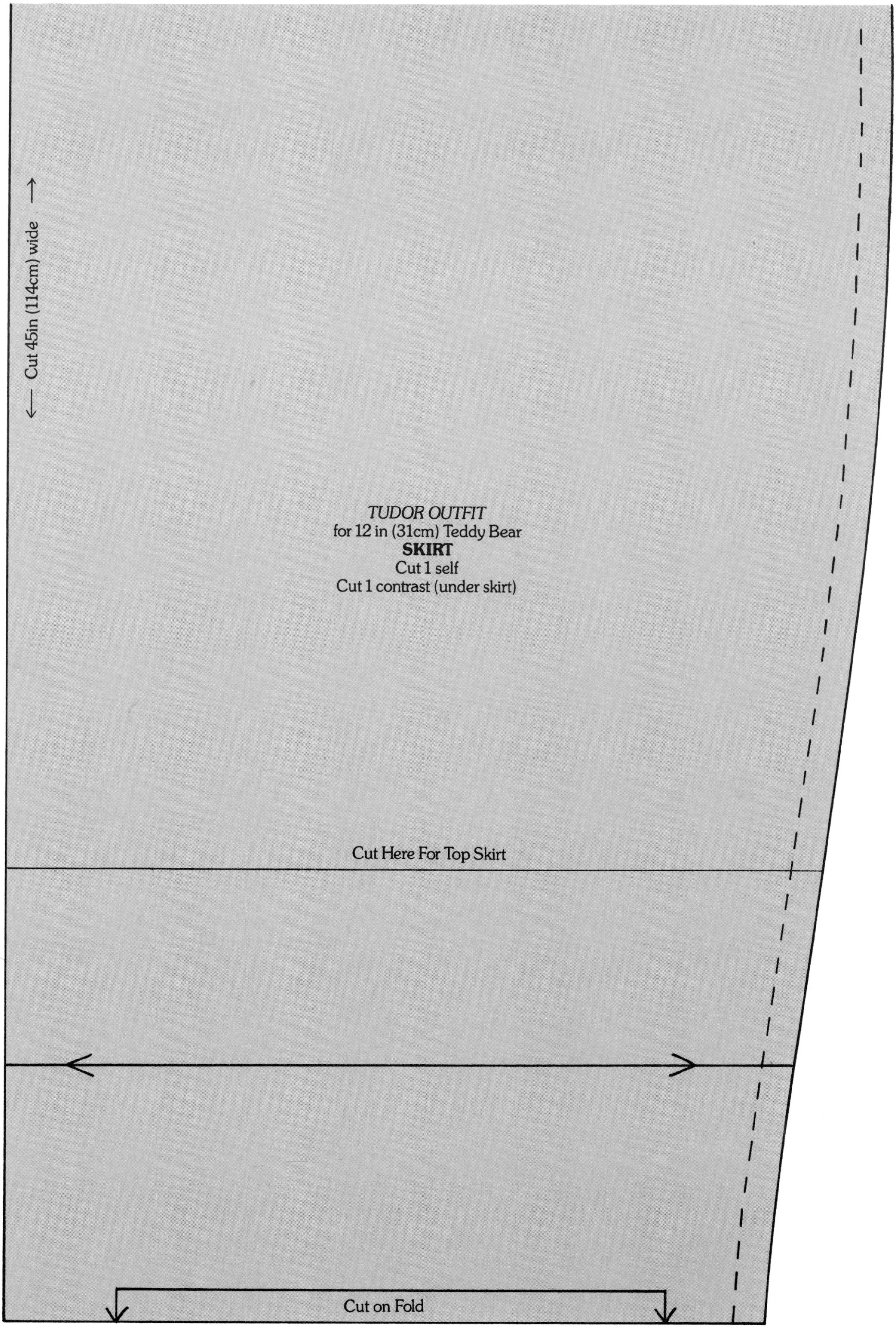

← Cut 45in (114cm) wide →

TUDOR OUTFIT
for 12 in (31cm) Teddy Bear
SKIRT
Cut 1 self
Cut 1 contrast (under skirt)

Cut Here For Top Skirt

Cut on Fold

Patterns continued on page 21

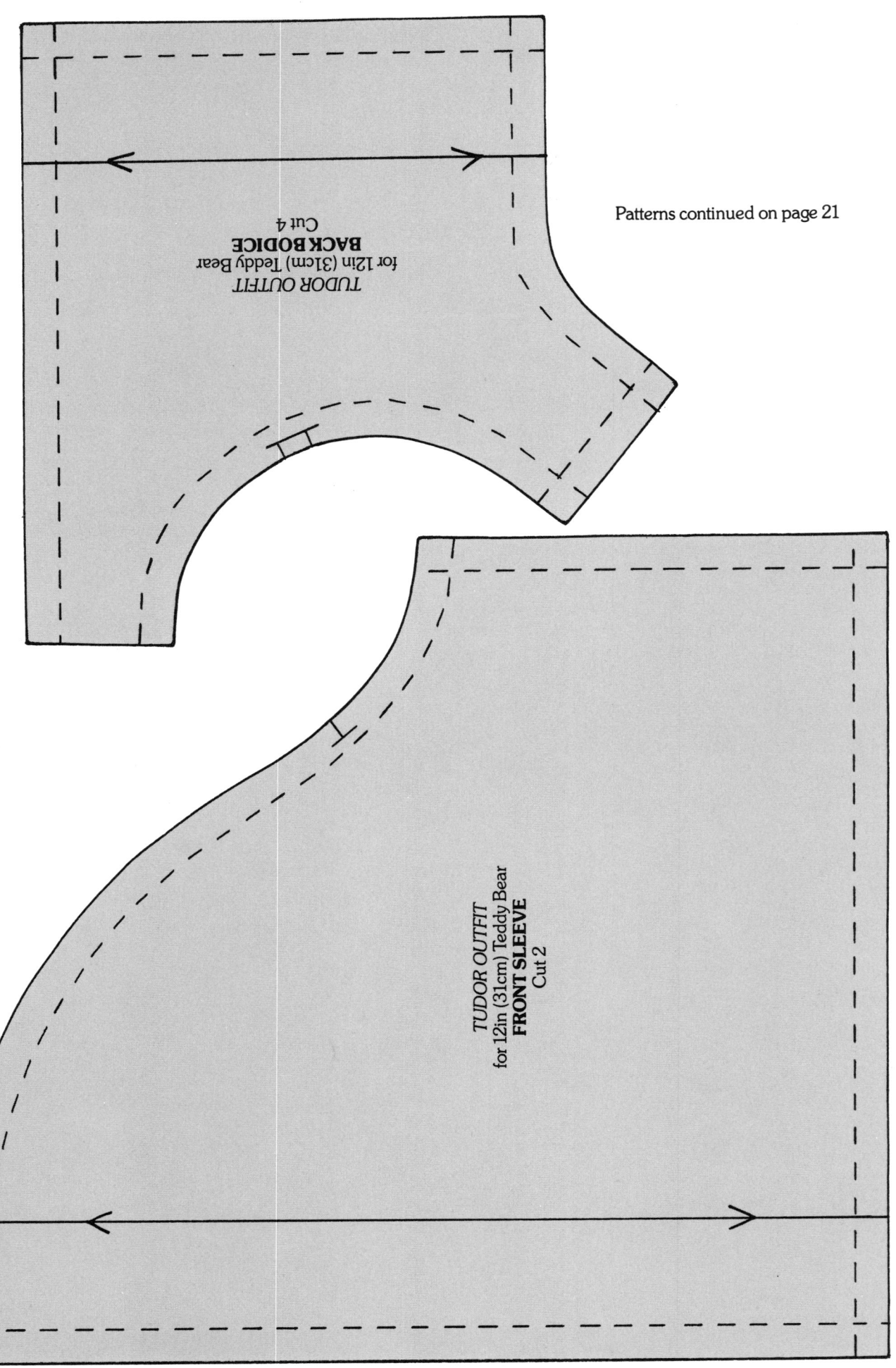

Patterns continued from page 16

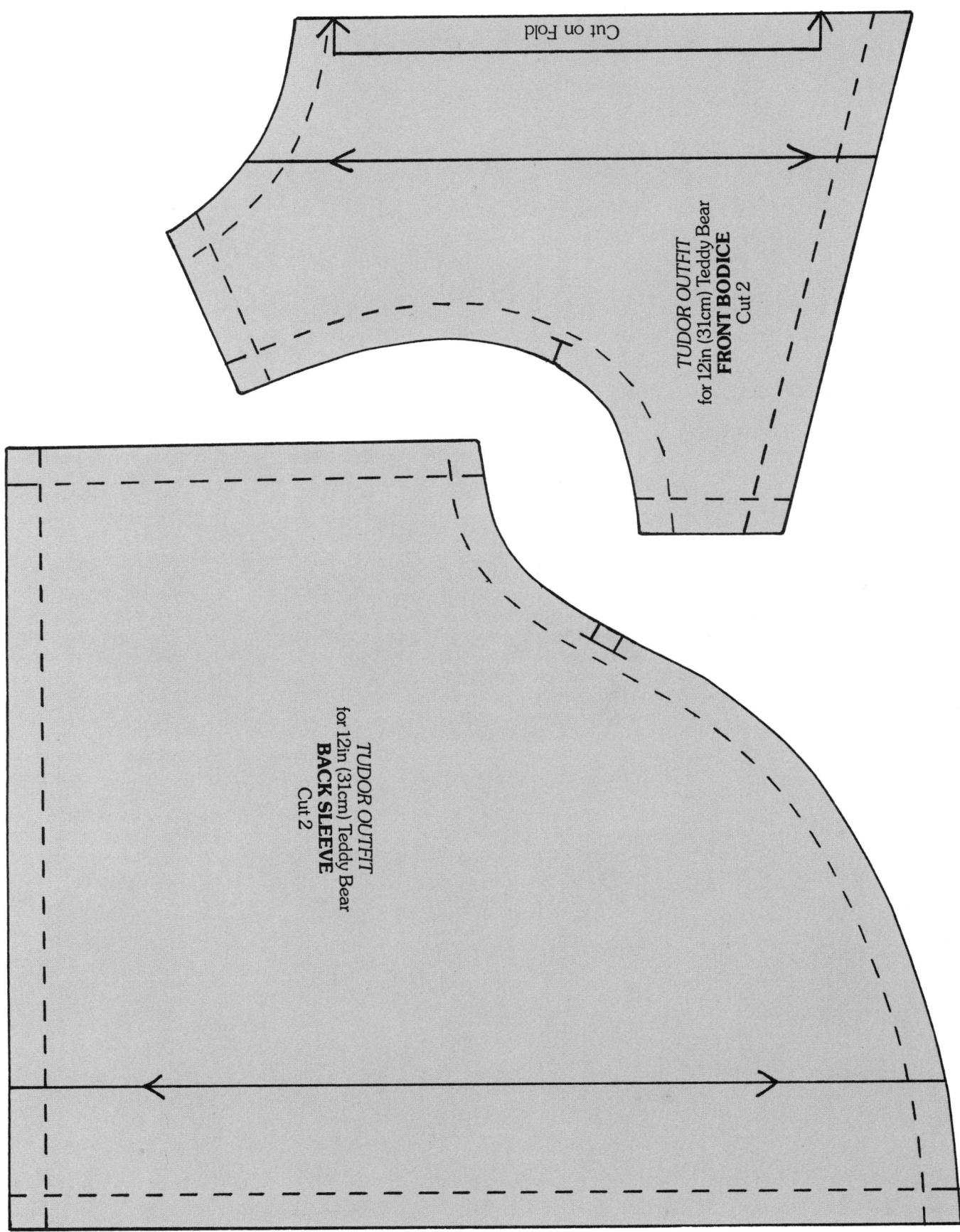

ELIZABETHAN MAN OUTFIT

This 12in (31cm) Steiff Teddy Bear is dressed in a lightweight synthetic suede type fabric with trim and tights and topped off with a beret.

FABRIC AND NOTIONS:
45in (114cm) fabric (pants, tunic/shirt) 1/2yd (46cm)
Felt (beret) . . . . 1 square
Stretch fabric (tights, end of sleeve) 1/4yd (23cm)
3/8in (.9cm) grosgrain ribbon (pants, tunic) . . . 6yd (549cm)
1in (2cm) wide bias (tunic) 1 1/2yd (137cm)
3/8in (0.9cm) grosgrain ribbon (waist tie, beret) 1yd (91cm)
1/4in (.65cm) elastic 1yd (91cm)
Snaps (back tunic) 4
Thread to match

PANTS:
1. Sew the grosgrain ribbon onto the pants at the markings. (See pattern.)
2. Sew the front and back seams. Press.
3. Sew the crotch seam. Clip curves at crotch. Press.
4. Press waist and pant leg hems under 1/8in (.31cm). Turn under again 1/2in (1cm) and stitch, leaving an opening to insert elastic. Insert 10in (25cm) into the waist and 5in (13cm) into each pant leg. Stitch ends of elastic closed and close the opening.

TUNIC/SHIRT:
1. Sew the grosgrain ribbon onto the front tunic at the markings. (See the pattern.)
2. Sew the shoulder seams together on the self and lining. Press seams open.
3. Sew the bias onto the lower tunic. You can slip the hem edges inside the fold on one end of the bias and stitch in place. Be sure to sew the middle piece of bias on before you stitch the upper edge of the bias.
4. Baby hem the side seams on the lower tunic on the front and back and also on the center back. Leave the waist alone.
5. Sew the lower tunic to the upper self tunic. The lower pieces will fall 1/4in (.65cm) short on the sides and at the center back.
6. With right sides facing, sew the lining to self. Sew up center back, around the neck and back down center back on the other side. Sew across the waist seams (with lower tunic inside so that when turned the waist will be clean). Clip, turn and press.
7. Sew the bias to the sleeves.
8. Shirr the sleeve to meet the armhole. Sew the sleeve into the armhole.
9. Shirr the lower sleeve to fit the cuff.
10. Fold the cuff in half and sew the sleeve to the cuff with raw edges together.
11. Sew the side seams. Zigzag seam. Press.
12. Sew the snaps onto the back tunic.

BERET:
1. Shirr the edge of the circle to measure 9in (23cm).
2. Cut the grosgrain ribbon 1/2in (1cm) larger and stitch the ends with 1/4in (.65cm) seam allowance. Sew the ribbon to the circle over the shirring stitch.
3. Pin the beret to the bear's head when he wears it.

TIGHTS:
1. With right sides facing, sew center front and center back seams together. Stretch as you sew.
2. Sew around the feet and crotch; stretch as you sew.
3. Fold waist down 1/2in (1cm) and stitch 3/8in (1cm) from the top leaving an opening for the elastic. Insert 10in (25cm) of elastic into the waist. Stitch ends of elastic. Stitch opening closed.

BELT:
1. Cut grosgrain ribbon long enough to tie around your bear's waist. Lay the ribbon over the waist seam on the front and tie in the back.

Dress your bear in his new Elizabethan costume and get out your Shakespeare for him to read.

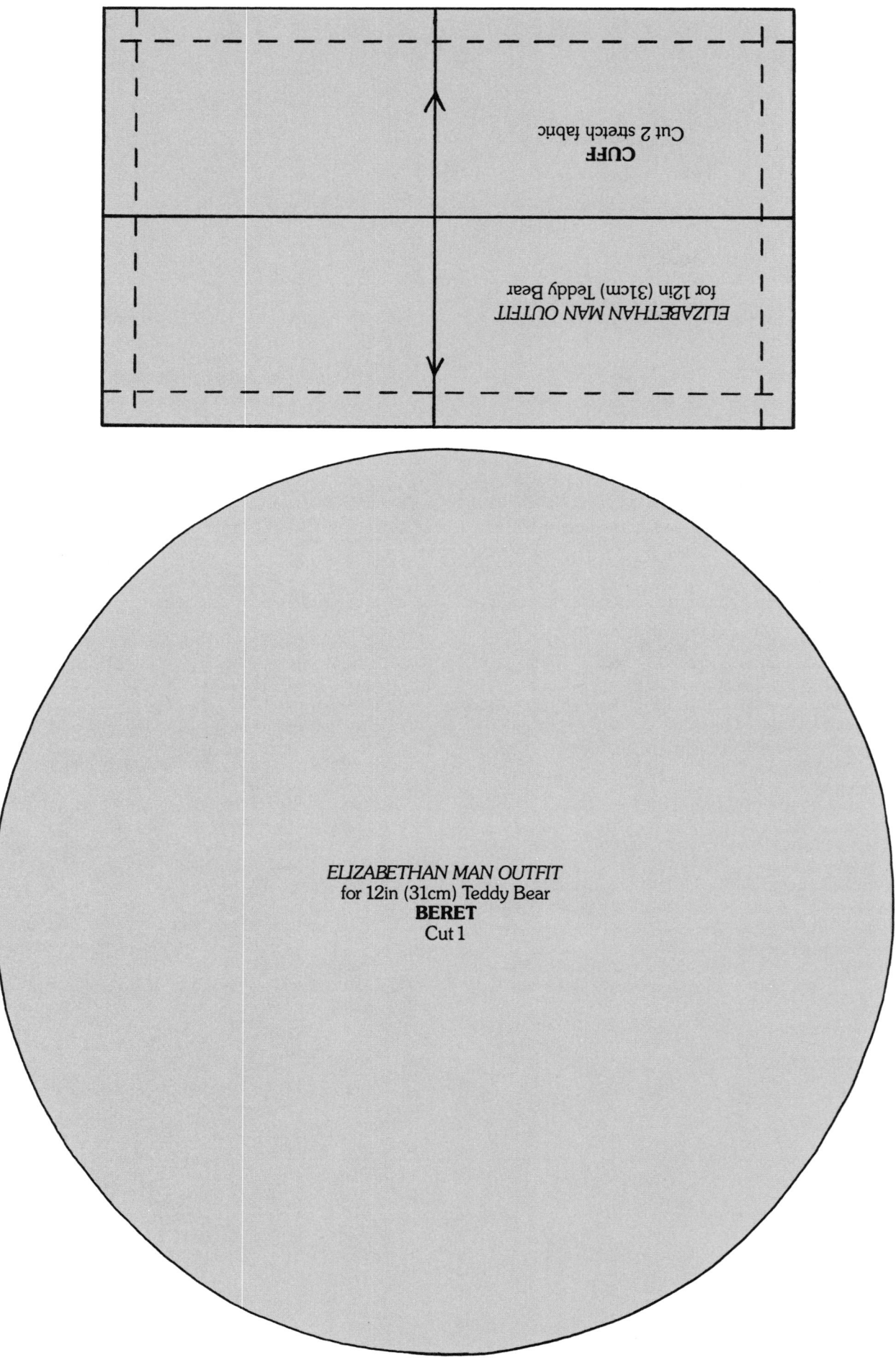

ELIZABETHAN MAN OUTFIT
for 12in (31cm) Teddy Bear
PANTS
Cut 2

Cut on Fold

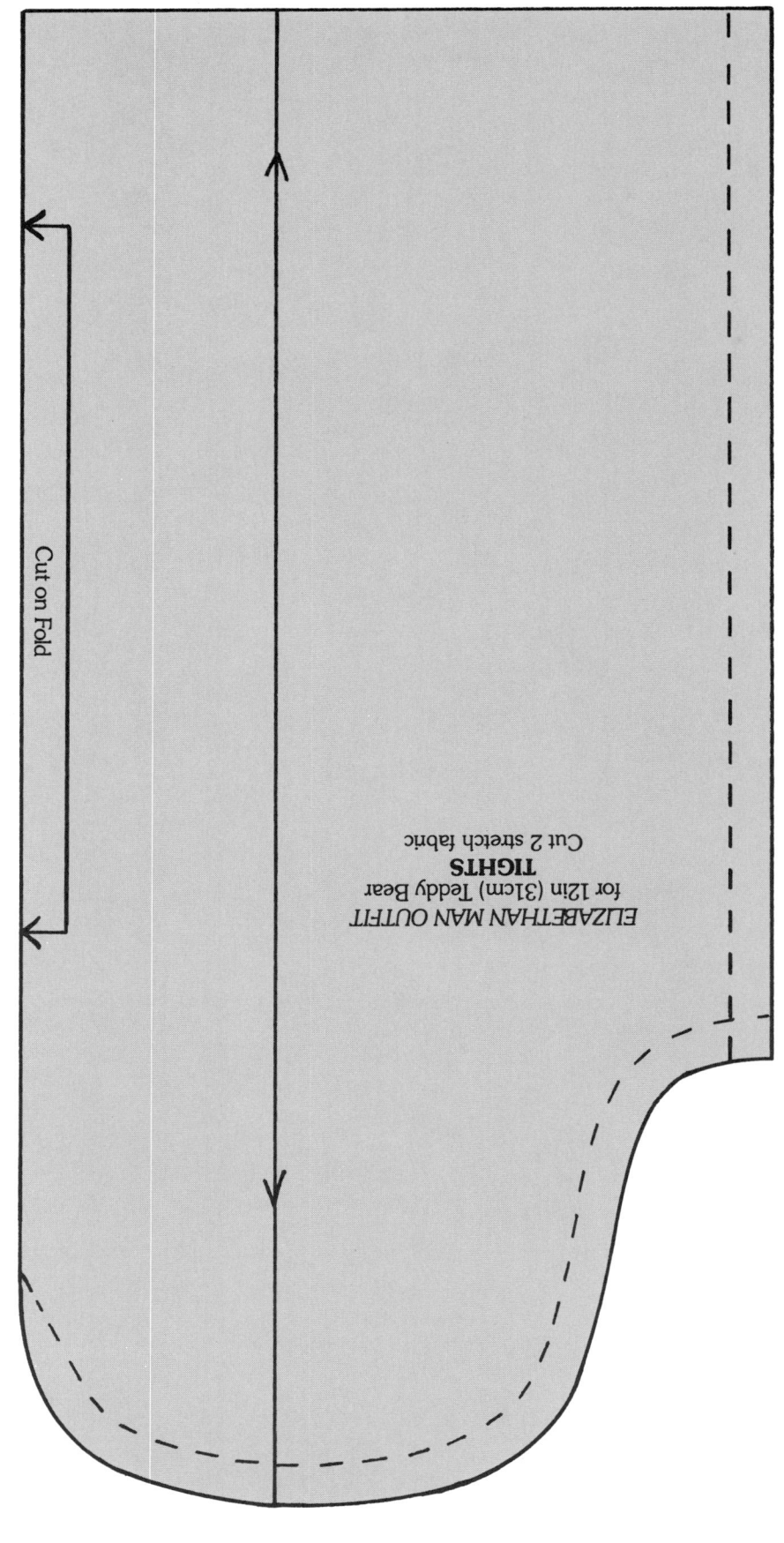

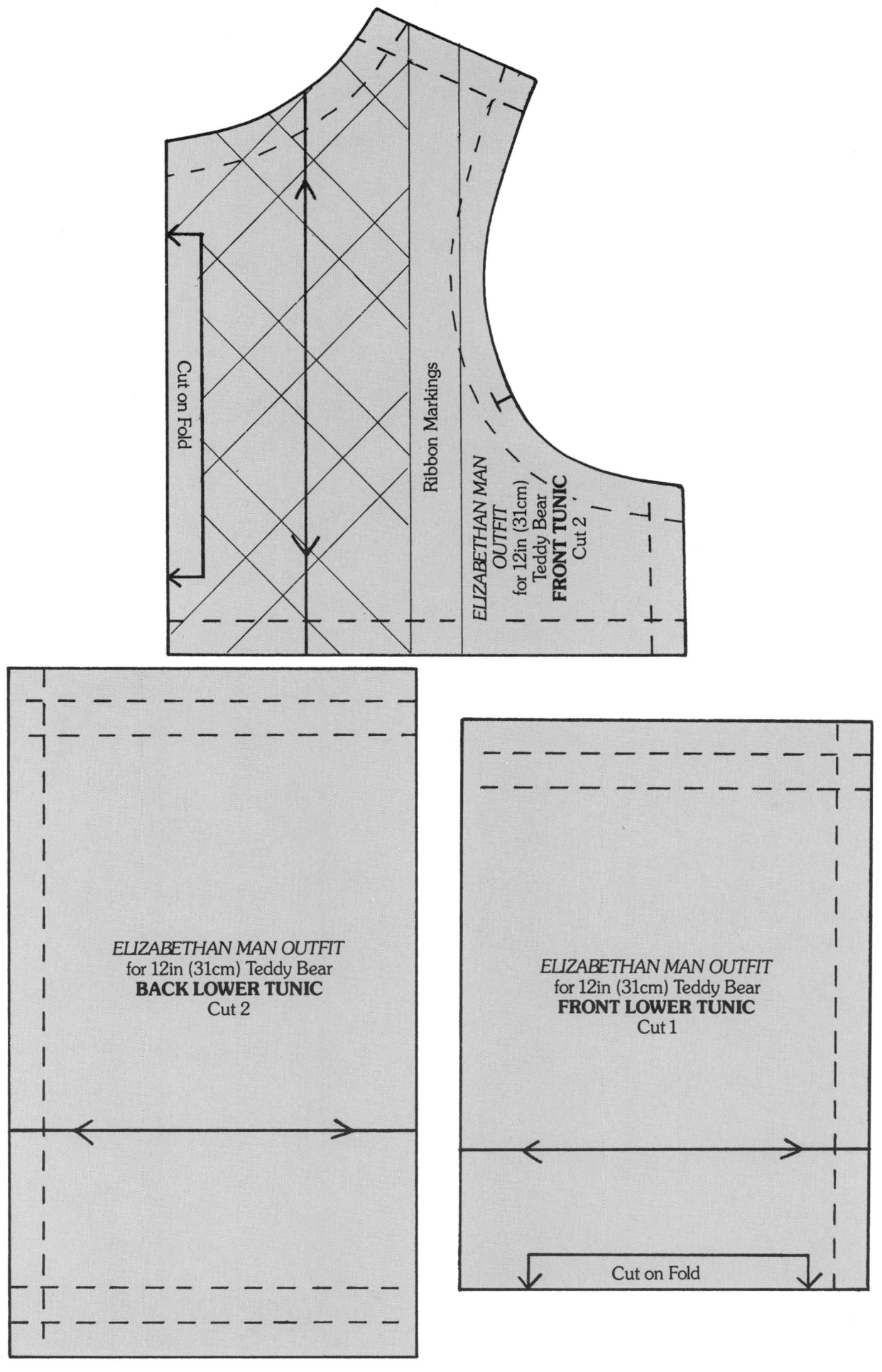

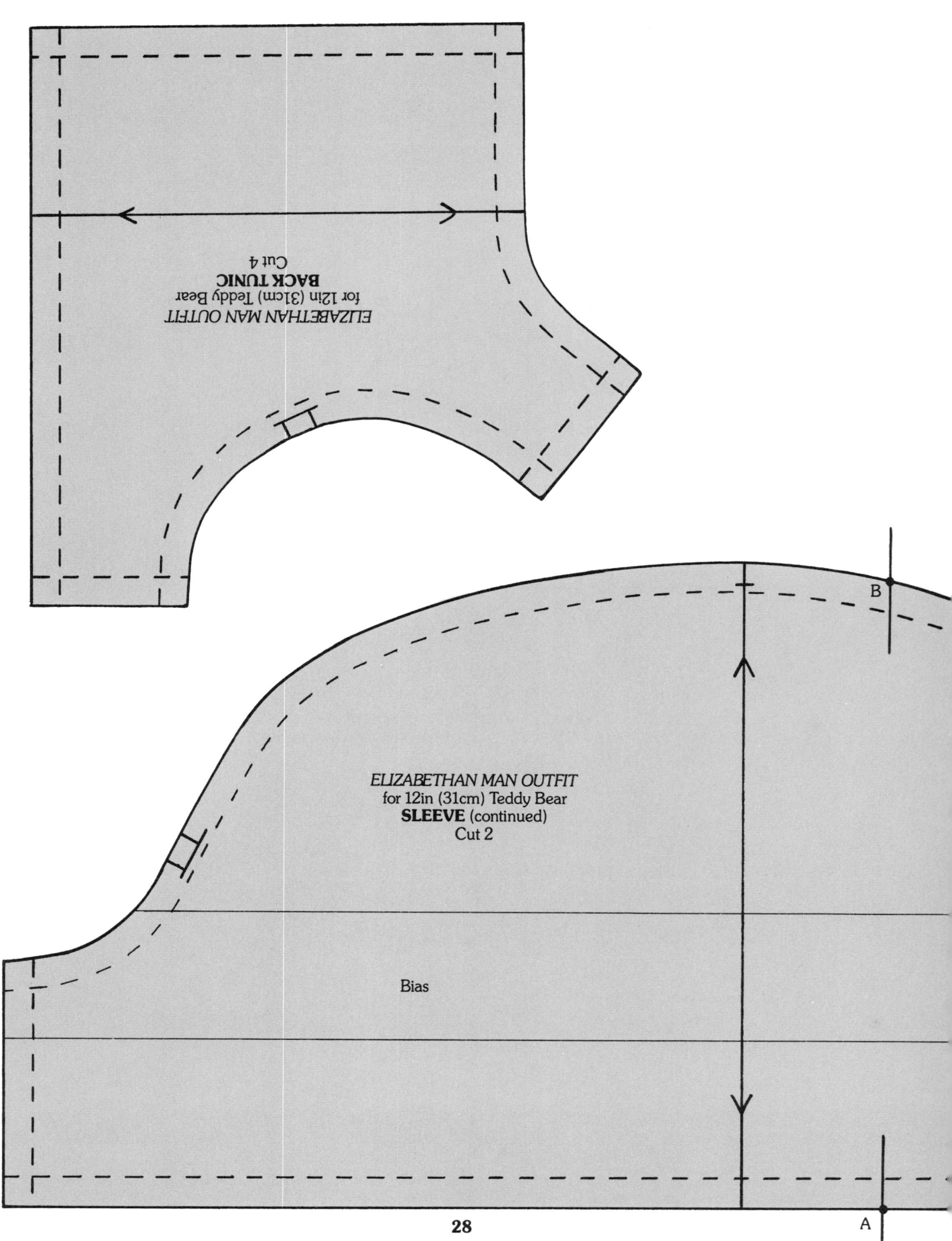

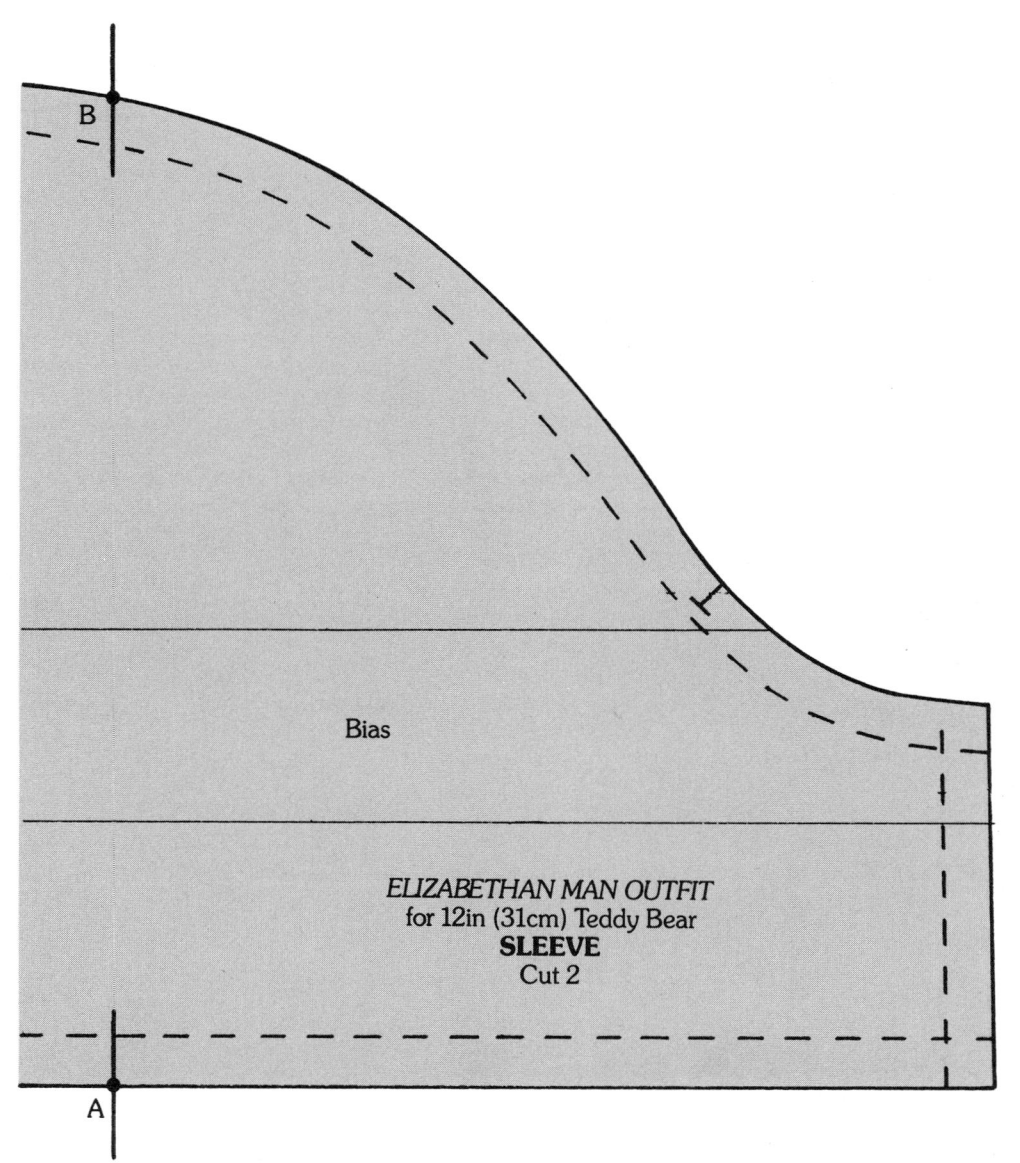

FRENCH 18TH CENTURY OUTFIT

This 12in (31cm) Steiff Teddy Bear is wearing a tapestry suit with trim.

FABRIC AND NOTIONS:

45in (114cm) tapestry fabric	3/4yd (69cm)
45in (114cm) taffeta lining	1/3yd (31cm)
Foldover bias	1/2yd (46cm)
Snaps/buttons	3
1/4in (.65cm) ribbon (neck)	1/2yd (46cm)
45in (114cm) fabric (neck scarf)	1/4yd (23cm)
1¼in (3cm) lace (cuffs)	1/2yd (46cm)
3/8in (.9cm) lace (jacket and vest)	2½yd (229cm)
1/4in (.65cm) elastic	1/2yd (46cm)
Baby socks	1 pair
Thread to match	
1/8in (.31cm) elastic	1/4yd (23cm)

PANTS:
1. Sew front and back seams together. Press.
2. Sew the crotch seam together. Press. Clip around the curves on the crotch.
3. Zigzag the edges of the waist and the pant legs. Press both edges under 5/8in (2cm) and stitch in place leaving an opening for the elastic.
4. Insert 10in (25cm) of elastic into the waist and 5in (13cm) into each leg. Stitch the ends of the elastic and stitch the opening closed.

VEST:
1. With right sides facing, sew the shoulder seams together on the self and lining. Press.
2. With right sides facing, sew self to lining. Sew up center front, around the neck and back down center front on the other side. Sew across the hems. Trim, turn and press.
3. Sew foldover bias to the armhole to clean.
4. Since the front is longer than the back, clip to where the back seam meets the front side seam. Press excess back and hand-stitch in place. Sew the remaining side seam and zigzag.
5. Edge stitch the vest.
6. Sew trim on the edges.
7. Sew on the snaps to the front.
8. OPTION: Since this particular style has a fetish for buttons, you may wish to sew buttons onto the vest and also the jacket just as decoration. Check any historical costume book for ideas.

COAT:
1. Sew the center back seam on the self and the lining. Press.
2. Sew shoulder seams together on the self and lining. Press.
3. Make the pleats on the back coat on the self and lining. Use the pattern notches and press the pleats onto the fabric. Sew the pleated sections to the back coat, the lining to the lining and the self to the self.
4. Press the "pockets" on the seam allowance lines. (See the pattern.) Stitch the "pockets" onto the front coat with an edge stitch. Sew lace around the pocket on the outer edges.
5. Sew the sleeve into the armhole. There are tucks at the cap.
6. Fold the cuff in half and sew lace to the folded edge.
7. Sew cuff to the sleeve so the raw edges are inside the cuff on the outside. The end of the sleeve will be clean.
8. Sew the side seams on the self and the lining. Zigzag and press.
9. With right sides facing, sew lining to self. Start at the side seam hem, go up center front, around the neck and repeat on the other side. Clip, turn and press.
10. Sew the armhole lining to the self armhole.
11. Turn up the back hems on the self and lining and baby hem separately. Repress the pleats at the edges.
12. Sew lace around the jacket.

NECK RUFFLE:
1. Baby hem all the edges.
2. 1/2in (1cm) down on one long edge shirr to 6in (15cm).
3. Sew the ribbon on top of the shirring, leaving equal amounts on each end to tie at the back of the bear's neck.

SLEEVE RUFFLE:
1. Stretch and sew 1/8in (.3cm) elastic to the top of the wide lace. Stitch the ends to form a cuff.
2. After the bear is dressed, slip the lace cuffs on the bear's wrist so they will show under the sleeve.

SOCKS:
1. Slip the socks onto the bear first thing when dressing him and they will probably pull up his entire leg. Then dress him in the rest of his outfit.

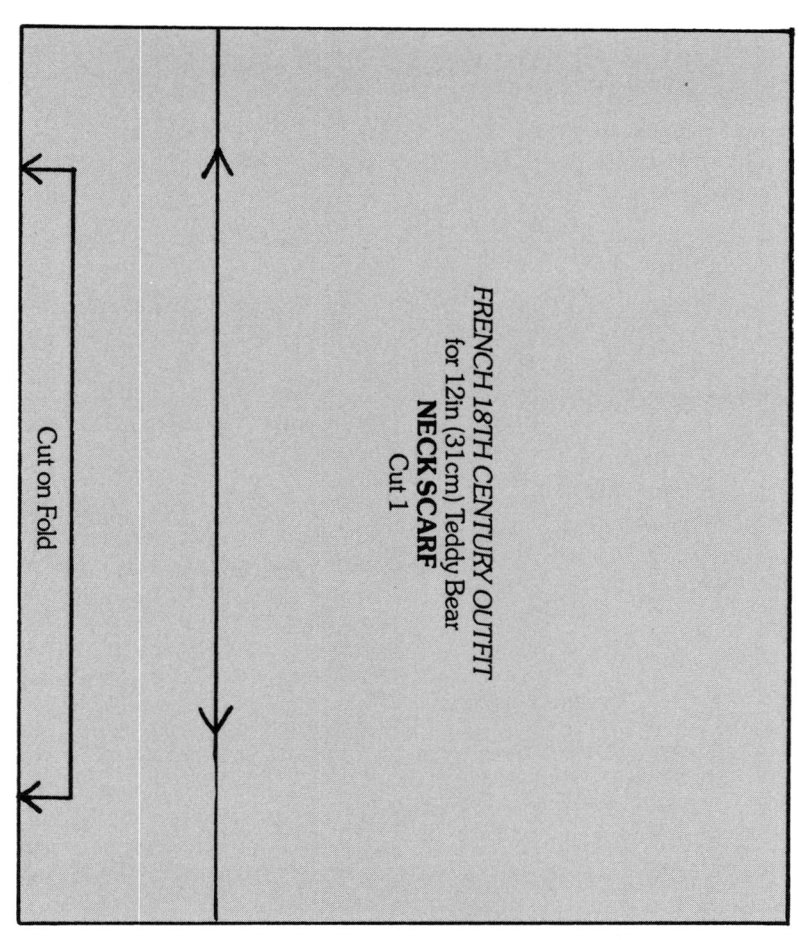
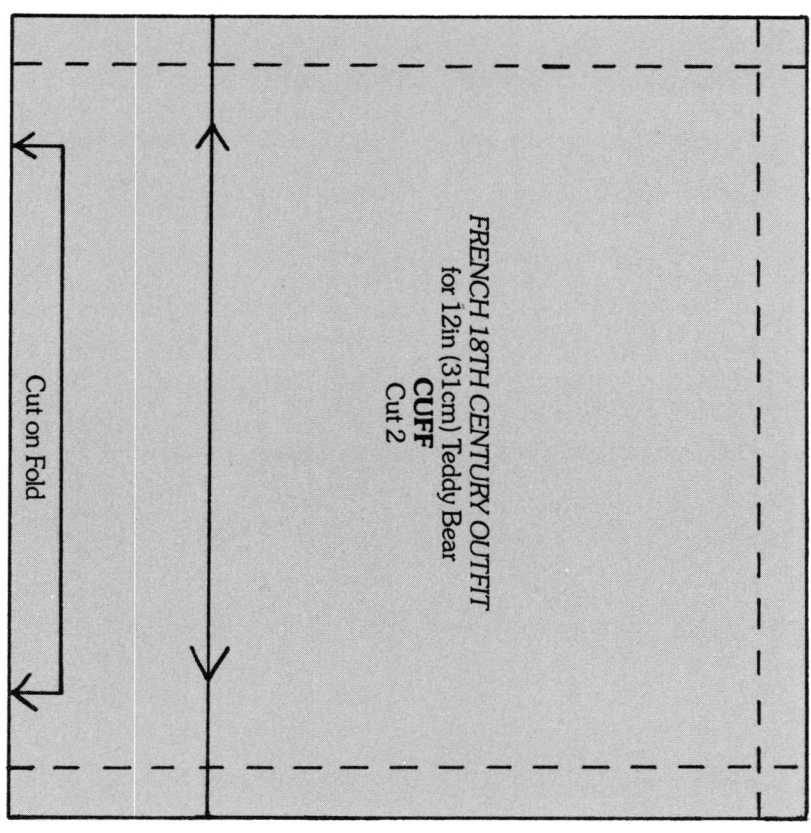

FRENCH 18TH CENTURY OUTFIT
for 12in (31cm) Teddy Bear
BACK JACKET PLEATS
Cut 1 self
Cut 1 lining
Cut on Fold

FRENCH 18TH CENTURY OUTFIT
for 12in (31cm) Teddy Bear
PANTS
Cut 2
Cut on Fold

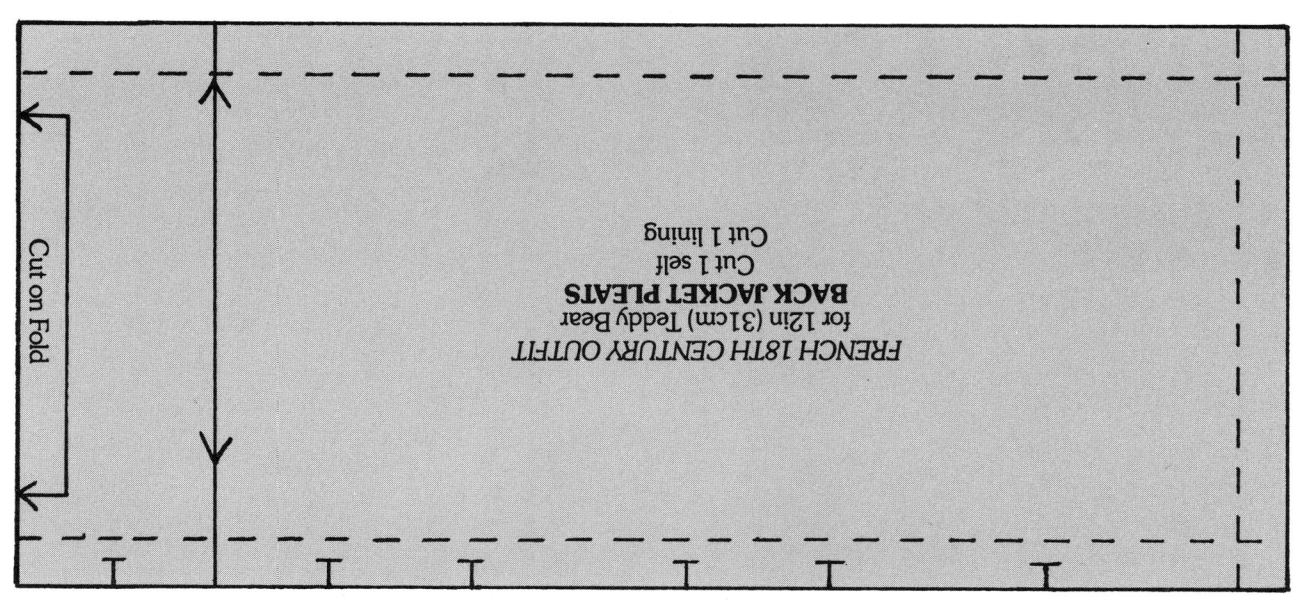

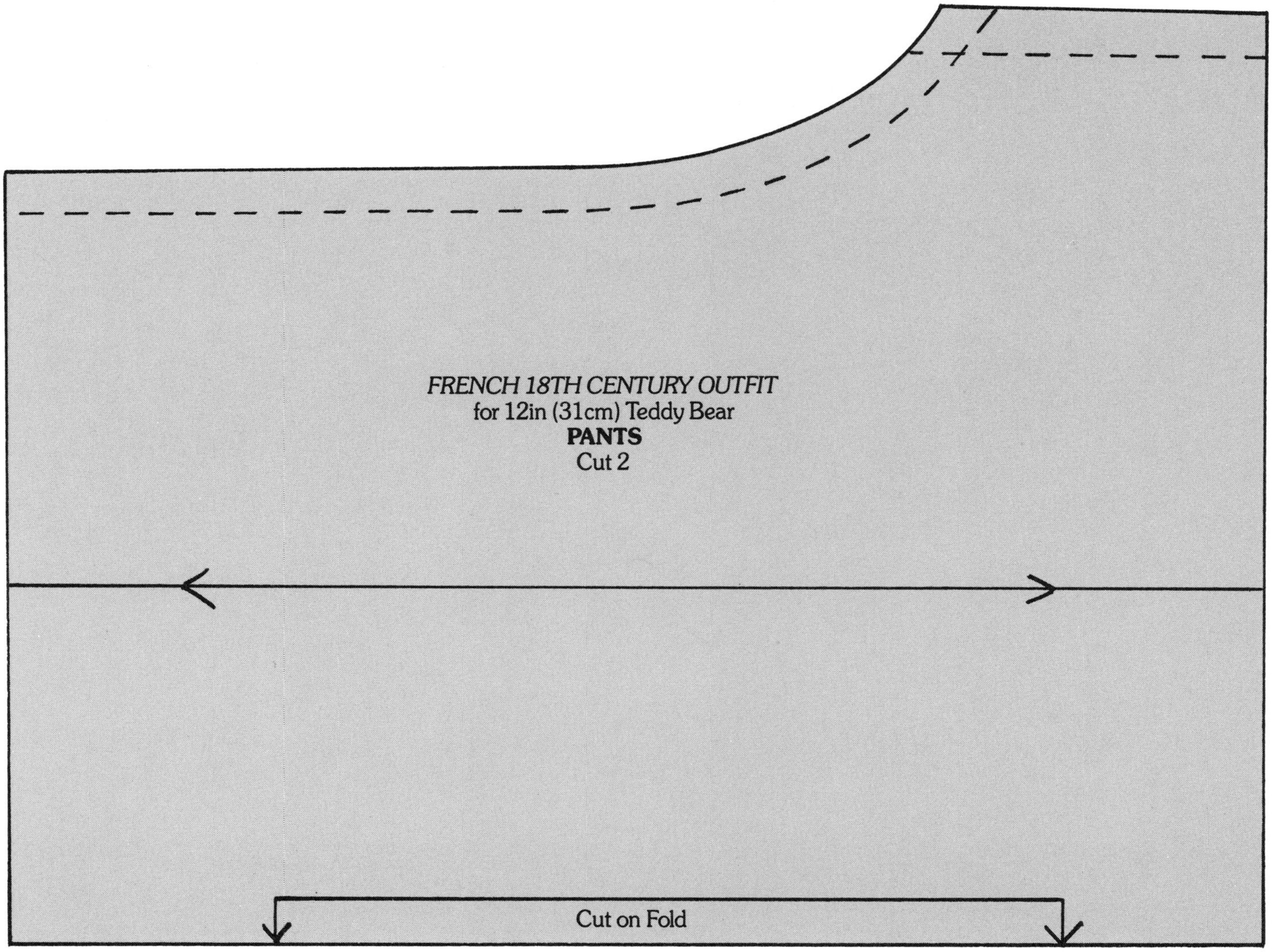

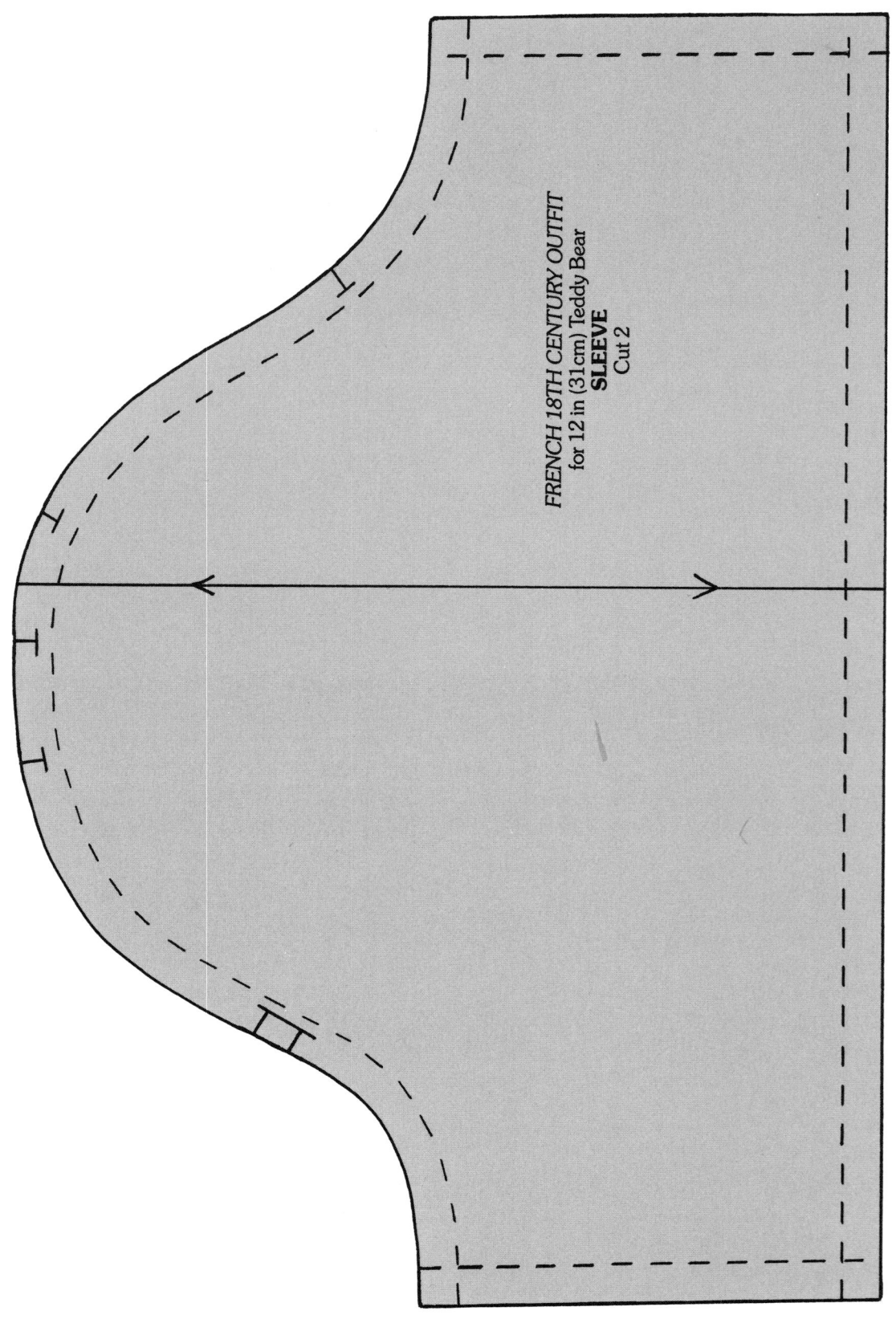

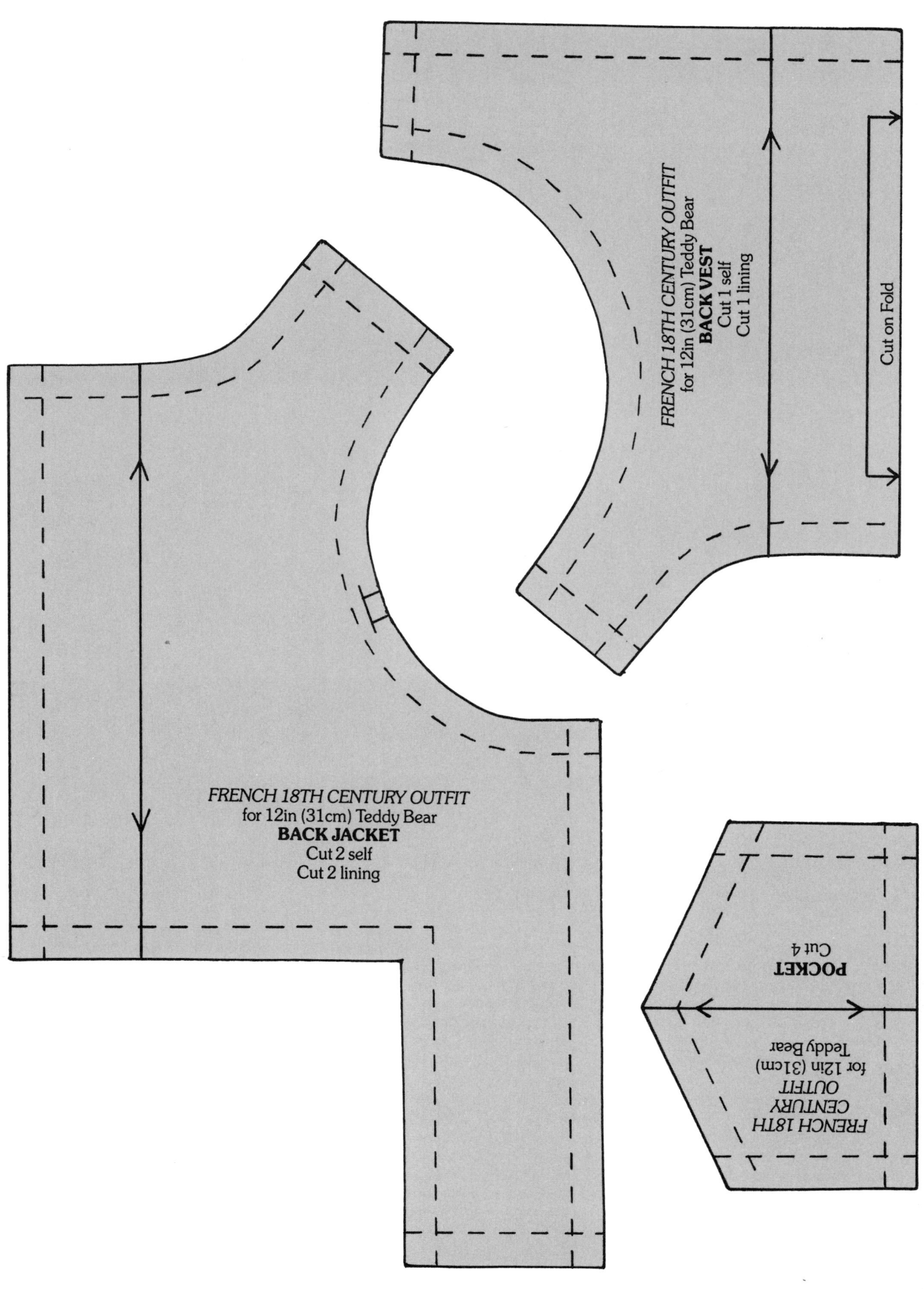

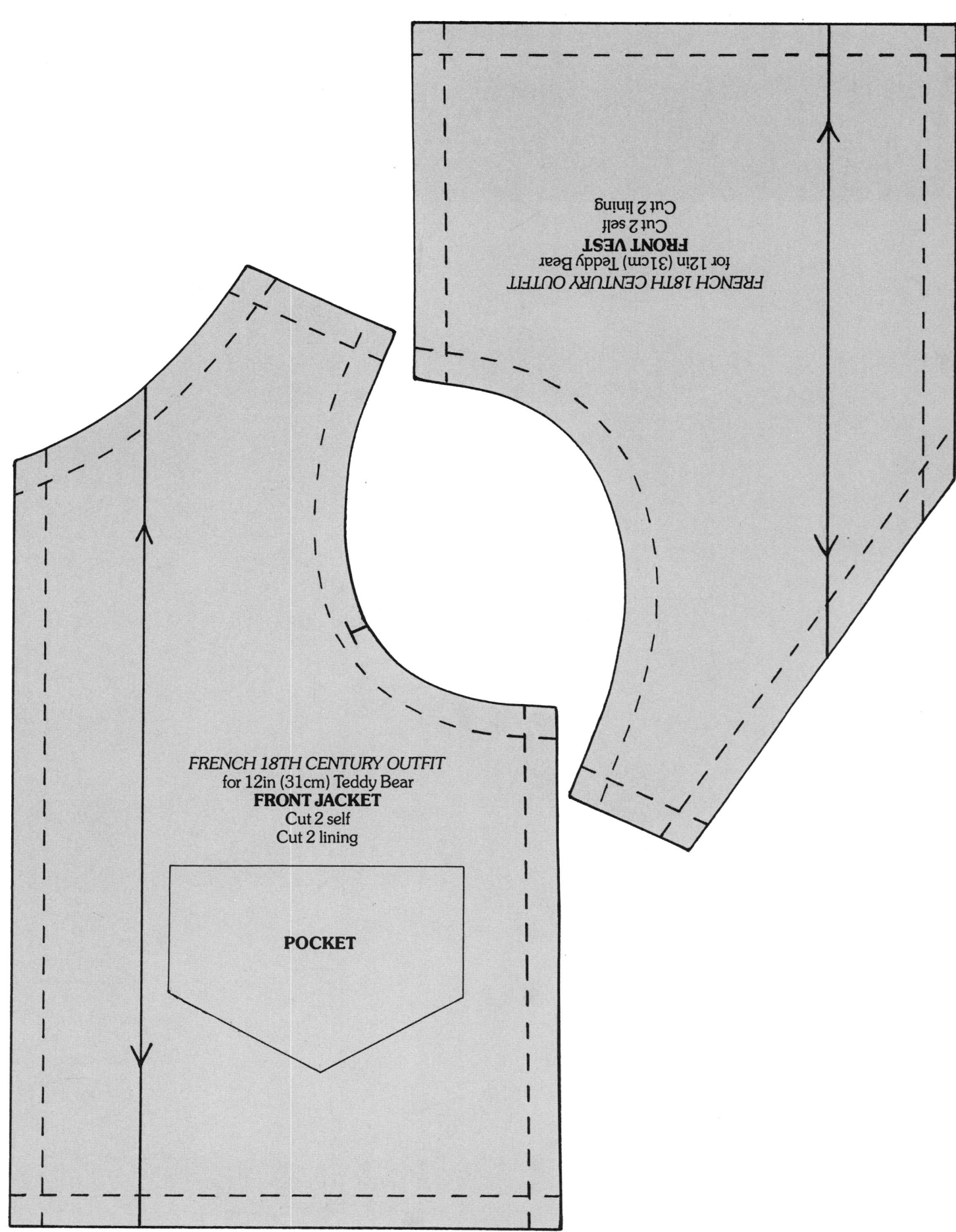